D0817374

The dynamic duo of Dr. Laurie Capogna and Dr. Barbara Pelletier co-wrote the bestselling adult book *Eyefoods: A Food Plan for Healthy Eyes*. They are passionate about food and eye health and they speak on these subjects at events and conferences. This is their first book for young readers.

For more about the doctors and eyefoods, see www.eyefoods.com

Dr. Barbara Pelletier

A native of Jonquiere, Quebec, Dr. Barbara Pelletier took up photography at age 14, sparking a lifelong interest in cameras and the visual system. She studied optometry at university and now works as an eye doctor. Dr. Pelletier enjoys cooking, staying active, and spending time with her favorite portrait subjects — her husband and daughters.

Dr. Laurie Capogna

Dr. Laurie Capogna grew up on an Ontario fruit and vegetable farm. She later attended university, became an optometrist (eye doctor), and developed an interest in the links between good food, nutrition, and eye health. Dr. Capogna enjoys experimenting in the kitchen, swimming with her nieces and nephews, and traveling to wacky places.

eyefoods® for kids

A Tasty Guide to Nutrition and Eye Health

DR. LAURIE CAPOGNA, OD & DR. BARBARA PELLETIER, OD

LB Media Concepts Inc.

www.eyefoods.com

Developed by: LB Media Concepts
Editorial: Ellen Rodger, Plan B Book Packagers
Design: Rosie Gowsell-Pattison, Plan B Book Packagers
Proofreader: Carrie Gleason

Photographs:
Robert Nowell: p. 2 (top), back cover (bottom).
Dr. Barbara Pelletier: p. 9, p. 16, pp. 22-23, p. 32 (bottom), p. 34 (top), p. 35 (top left and right), p. 37.
Kathy White, Absolute Image Photography: p. 2 (bottom), back cover (top).
All other images from Shutterstock.com

Illustrations:
Margaret Amy Salter: p. 8, pp. 10-11, p. 15, p. 30.

For bulk sales to schools, organizations, and health-related companies, email us at info@eyefoods.com

Teachers and educators: if you would like information on integrating Eyefoods for Kids into the classroom, please email us at info@eyefoods.com

Library and Archives Canada Cataloging in Publication
Capogna, Laurie
    Eyefoods for kids : a tasty guide to nutrition and eye health / Laurie Capogna & Barbara Pelletier.

Includes index.
ISBN 978-0-9868079-3-0

    1. Eye--Diseases--Diet therapy. 2. Eye--Care and hygiene. 3. Diet therapy for children. I. Pelletier, Barbara II. Title.

RE991.C363 2013   617.7'0654   C2013-901700-3

Printed and bound in the United States.

contents

A Lifetime of Sight

Imagine what life would be like without vision. We use our eyes every day for almost every task we do.

Our sight is one of the human body's five senses. In our visual system, we use our eyes to "see" or gather information. This information is sent to our brains where it is decoded.

Our visual system is incredible and our sense of sight is precious! We see objects near and far, in color and black and white, and in slow and fast motion. We also see in **three dimensions** instead of flat pictures. Our eyes (and brain) allow us to do all this, yet we often take them for granted.

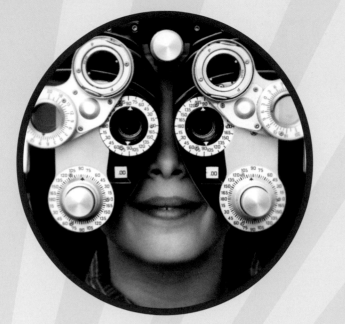

fun fact

Did you know that needing to wear glasses does not mean you have unhealthy eyes? Eyeglasses are used for eyes that cannot focus light properly. Unhealthy eyes have diseases and may need medication or surgery to make them better.

There are many simple things we can do to keep our eyes healthy. Diet, exercise, and eye protection are very important to our vision. Eating certain foods can help prevent eye disease and keep our eyes healthy for our entire lives. We need vitamins, minerals, healthy fats, and plant **pigments** called carotenoids, to maintain healthy eyesight.

How the Eye Works

Our eyes are amazing organs made up of many parts. Each part does a different job.

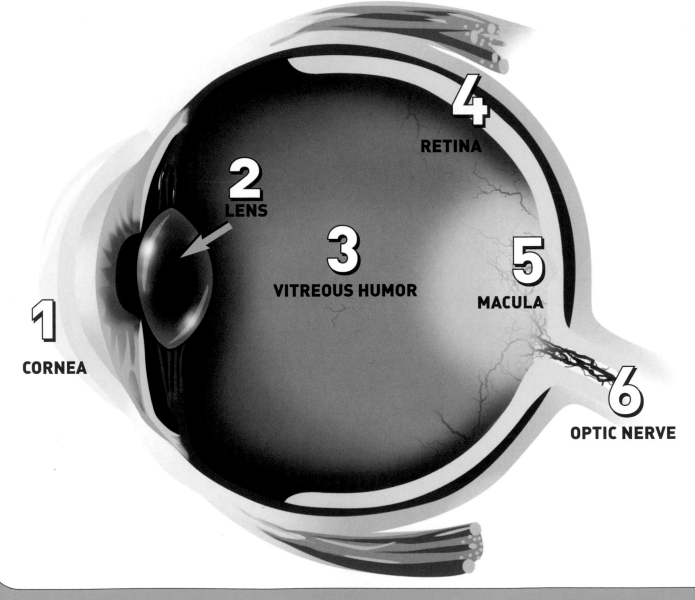

1. The **CORNEA** is the clear outer part of the eye. It helps refract, or change the direction of, light coming into the eye. This aids in focusing.

2. The **LENS** is located behind the iris. Both the lens and the cornea focus light and images on the retina.

3. The **VITREOUS HUMOR** is located in the longest part of the eye and looks and feels like jelly. It is transparent, which means it allows light to pass through it.

4. The **RETINA** is the tissue that lines the back of the eye. It converts light into electrical impulses that are sent to the brain.

5. The **MACULA** in the center of the retina, allows for detailed central vision, or seeing straight ahead.

6. Located at the back of the eye, the **OPTIC NERVE** sends messages to the brain. The brain then interprets what the eye sees.

7. The **SCLERA**, also known as the white of the eye, is the tough outer coating. Six muscles connected to it control the eye's movement.

8. The **PUPIL** is the dark part at the center of the iris. It is actually a hole. Light enters the eye here. When it is bright, the pupil is small. When it is dark, the pupil grows bigger to let in more light.

9. The **IRIS** is the colored part of the eye. It controls the amount of light that enters the eye by opening and closing the pupil.

How Does Vision Work?

Have you ever wondered how your eyes "see"? Sight is one of your most important senses. But how you see is not as simple as you might think. You don't just see with your eyes. You see with your brain too.

1 The object you are looking at bounces light.

2 Light passes through the cornea. The pupil changes size to adjust how much light comes in. Light then passes through the clear lens. Both the cornea and the lens are curved so the light bends, helping it reach a specific point on the retina. The magnification power of the lens is so high that it inverts, or flips, the image.

3 Light focuses at the macula and the macula creates the vision signal. The macula is located in the center of the retina and is responsible for central vision, or seeing in front. It allows you to see in detail and do things such as reading.

3

5

5 Like a computer, the brain's visual cortex "processes," or sorts through, information. The information (an image) is received upside down through the visual cortex. The visual cortex flips it right side up.

4

The brain's cells receive information from both your right eye and your left eye. Some brain cells see from the right eye and some from the left eye. Some see from both eyes together. This is why you see better with both eyes open. The brain matches and blends the image received from both eyes together.

4 The vision signal is passed through the optic nerve to the visual cortex.

Eyes to Brain

Have you ever noticed how a friend's pupils change size depending on the light? Sometimes they are as small as pinheads. Other times they are very wide. This is because the iris muscle surrounding our pupils controls the amount of light that enters the eye. Once light is focused on the retina, it is converted into signals by cells. These signals travel from the retina to the brain through the optic nerve. The brain then makes images based on the signals sent from the eyes.

The pupil is the black hole at the center of the iris. We have small pupils in bright light and large pupils in dim light. The pupil also becomes large when we are excited or afraid.

Rods and Cones

The retina has millions of **cells**. These cells are light-sensitive and are called rods and cones. Rods work in dim light and allow us to see black and white. Cones are cells that allow us to see colors in bright light.

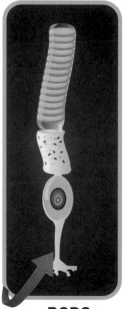

RODS   **CONES**

Our eyes have more rod cells than cone cells. Rods let us see in a dark room, while cones provide vision in good light.

fun fact

Humans have round eye pupils. Other animals, such as house cats, have vertical slit pupils that appear to be up and down. Tigers, lions, jaguars, and leopards have pupils that contract, or get smaller, to a round point. These animals are all predators, or hunters. The eyes of predators, including humans, can focus rapidly. Their pupils contract and dilate according to the light available. This allows them to see —and hunt—in bright or dim light. Animals that aren't hunters, such as goats, cattle, deer, and sheep, have horizontal pupils, which give them better vision to detect predators.

Vision and Learning

Almost 80 percent of what you learn begins with your sight. What you see makes up a lot of what you know.

Many things need to happen in the eye and the brain to have good vision for learning and playing. You need to have clear central vision, good eye-muscle strength, the ability to focus, and the ability to understand depth.

Clear Central Vision

Central vision is what you see from the center of your eyes. Clear central vision depends on the light being focused precisely at the eye's macula. The macula is the round yellow spot located in the center of the retina. It is important that you keep the macula healthy.

People often squint when they cannot see clearly. One cause of blurry vision is astigmatism. This happens when the cornea and/or lenses are shaped like cylinders instead of spheres. It can be corrected with glasses or contact lenses.

CLEAR VISION

The light entering the eye focuses on the macula and "hits the target" resulting in a clear image.

NEARSIGHTED VISION (MYOPIA)

The light entering the eye focuses in front of the macula and misses the target, resulting in blurry distance vision. Myopia often occurs when the eyeball is too long. Myopia can be corrected with glasses or contacts.

FARSIGHTED VISION (HYPEROPIA)

The light entering the eye focuses beyond the macula, resulting in blurry close-up vision. This makes reading difficult. Hyperopia happens when the eyeball is too short or the lens is not round enough. It can be corrected by wearing glasses or contacts.

Team Strength: Eye Muscle Coordination

The muscles that surround your eyes help you to focus your vision so that you can "see straight." Each eye has six **extraocular muscles**. They work as a team to aim both eyes at the object you are looking at. Like all of your body's muscles, they must be strong to work well. If there is a weakness in any of these muscles, the eyes won't coordinate, or work well together. Muscle weakness can cause double vision, jumbled sight, or amblyopia (lazy eye). If an eye weakness is very severe, the eye might turn in or out. This is called strabismus.

Not only do you need both eyes aiming at an object, you also need your eyes to hold their position on an object. Looking at something up close is the most **challenging**, or difficult, for eye muscles. Your eyes have to turn inward, or go crossed to do this. This is called convergence.

When you read or look at something closely, your eyes need to converge, or turn in, for you to see properly.

In Focus

The lens of the eye is very powerful. It can change its shape and how much it bends light. When you look at something far away, your lens is relaxed. When you read or play video games, your lens is active. The muscles around the lens must work together for the lens to change shape. If your lens does not focus, reading will be difficult, or you may have trouble looking from near to far and far to near.

Depth perception allows you to see how far away a car is when you are crossing a street.

Understanding Depth

You need clear central vision in both eyes, good eye muscle coordination, and the ability to focus to see in three dimensions. Three-dimensional sight means you can determine distance and depth through two eyes. This is called depth perception. Depth perception helps you to catch a ball or pour a glass of water.

fun fact

You need depth perception to see and enjoy a 3-D movie.

Eye Health and Safety

Your eyes are important. You depend upon them for many things, but it is easy for you to take them for granted. Like the rest of your body, your eyes need **nourishment**, exercise, and rest to function best.

Healthy eyes are free from disease and injury. There are many eye diseases but some of the most common are blepharitis, conjunctivitis, glaucoma, cataracts, and diseases of the retina. Blepharitis is a condition where the eyelid becomes sensitive, red, or flaky. Conjunctivitis, sometimes called pink eye, is an **inflammation** of the lining that covers the eyeball. Glaucoma and cataracts are diseases that can lead to blindness if left untreated. Retinal diseases can also cause blindness as they damage the retina. Many eye diseases can be prevented or slowed by eating foods that are good for the eyes.

Eye injuries can be caused by sports or other accidents, or by unhealthy lifestyles. Some injuries can be prevented by wearing proper eye protection.

How a person with healthy vision sees.

How a person with cataracts sees.

How a person with a diseased macula sees.

Protecting Your Eyes: With Food

Did you know that some vegetables can help keep your eyes healthy? Dark green vegetables, such as kale and spinach, and orange vegetables, such as orange peppers, are especially good for vision health. These vegetables contain chemicals called carotenoids and other vitamins that help your eyes work. There are plenty of other foods that are important for the health of your eyes including fish, fruit, eggs, nuts, and even turkey.

"Green means go" when it comes to the color of foods that are good for eyesight.

Protecting Your Eyes: From Injury

When you play sports you wear protective equipment to make sure that you don't get hurt. It's also very important to protect your eyes from injury. Almost half of all eye injuries happen in sports. High-risk sports include baseball, hockey, football, basketball, lacrosse, tennis, wrestling, boxing, contact martial arts, and water polo. Ninety percent of eye injuries can be prevented by wearing eyewear or helmets with facemasks made from a material called polycarbonate. Your eye doctor can recommend the proper protective eyewear for you.

Eye injuries are a leading cause of blindness in children. Most eye injuries among kids aged eleven to fourteen happen when playing sports without eye protection.

Protecting Your Eyes: From The Sun

Just as you need to wear sunscreen to protect your skin from burning, you need to wear sunglasses to protect your eyes from the harmful effects of ultraviolet (UV) light. UV light rays are invisible rays of sunlight that can burn skin and damage eyes. To protect your eyes, wear sunglasses with UV400 protection or lenses that darken in the sun (photochromic lenses) everyday.

The Sun's rays are intense, even from millions of miles away. Try not to look directly at the Sun.

fun fact

Polarized lenses allow you to see through water. Wear polarized sunglasses when you go fishing to clearly see the fish swimming through the water. They also take away glare, giving you super sharp vision on land and water.

A Test for Your Eyes

So, you think you have perfect vision? Time to put it to the test! Eye exams given by eye doctors, called optometrists test your vision and your eye health. People can have "perfect" vision, but still not have perfect eye health. For this reason, optometrists recommend getting your eyes examined every year.

What Happens During an Eye Exam?

During an eye exam, an optometrist will check your vision and how your eyes work together using a number of tests. She or he will also make sure that your eyes are healthy. Using special equipment, an optometrist will look at the different parts of the eye.

Your optometrist will use a microscope to look at the parts of your eye and make sure they are healthy.

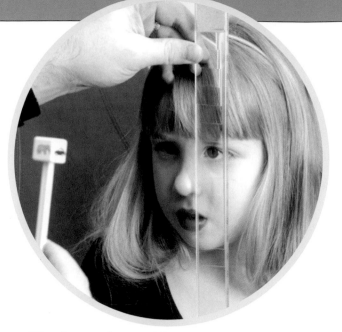

The doctor is checking to see how much strain your eyes can take before they see double.

Your optometrist will check how well you see with each eye.

fun fact

THE THREE O'S

OPTICIAN: An optician is an eye-care professional who is trained to design, fit, and sell eyeglasses and contact lenses.

OPTOMETRIST: An optometrist is a doctor of optometry who performs **comprehensive** eye examinations for their patients. They focus on all aspects of vision and overall eye health.

OPHTHALMOLOGIST: An ophthalmologist is a medical doctor who specializes in the diagnosis and treatment of eye diseases. Many ophthalmologists are also eye surgeons. They perform surgeries and laser treatments on the eye.

Contact Lenses and Glasses

Contact lenses and glasses correct vision by allowing the eyes to focus light correctly on the retina. Each eyeglass or contact **prescription** is specific to a person's vision issue. Try on a friend's or a parent's glasses. You may notice that they make you dizzy. This is because everyone's eyes are different and a vision correction for one person can **distort** the vision of another. Contact lenses correct vision by fitting right on the eye's cornea. They are medical devices that move with your eyes and are perfectly comfortable. As a result, no matter where you look, you always have clear vision. All contact lenses should be "fitted" on your eyes by an optometrist or optician. They will also teach you how to use and care for your contacts.

Glasses should be "adjusted" so that they sit well on your face.

Most contact lenses are soft and comfortable to wear.

What is 20/20 Vision?

People who have 20/20 vision are usually thought to have "normal" vision. But this does not mean perfect vision. A person with 20/20 vision should see what a normal person sees at 20 feet away. Eye doctors call this visual acuity, or sharpness of vision.

Optometrists use eye charts to test distance vision.

fun fact

Did you know that you blink 17 times in a minute? That's almost six million blinks a year. Blinking is especially important when you wear contact lenses to keep your vision clear and your eyes comfortable.

Feast Your Eyes on This!

Your eyes are meant to last a lifetime. Healthy eyes are eyes that are free from disease. But how can you keep your eyes disease free? One of the biggest contributors to eye health is your diet.

The foods you eat everyday are important because they provide the fuel for your entire body, including your eyes, to perform at its best. Your eyes and body need vitamins, minerals, omega-3 fatty acids, and other **nutrients** to work.

Leafy green vegetables and orange and yellow fruits and vegetables are packed with vitamins that keep your eyes healthy.

What is a Vitamin?

Vitamins come from plants and animals. Your body needs vitamins to develop, grow, and work well. Your body gets vitamins from the food you eat. Different foods contain different vitamins and some foods contain more vitamins than others. For example, vegetables and fruits contain many vitamins but chips and candy don't.

Candy is sweet for an occasional treat, but it contains no vitamins or minerals.

There are 13 vitamins. Some vitamins dissolve in water and some dissolve in fat. Your body cannot store the vitamins that dissolve in water, so you must eat food with these vitamins often. Vitamin C is a vitamin that dissolves in water. The vitamins that are most important to our eyesight are vitamin A, vitamin C and vitamin E.

Vegetables and salads are tasty and good for your eyes and the rest of your body.

What is a Mineral?

Minerals come from nature. They are found in earth, rocks, and water. When you eat plants and animals, the minerals they took from nature are passed on to you. This way your body gets the minerals it needs to grow and function properly.

Calcium, sodium (in salt), and zinc are examples of minerals that are used by your body. Your body uses calcium to build strong bones and teeth. Zinc is an important mineral for your eyes. It transfers vitamin A and vitamin E to your eyes from the liver where they are stored. Oysters contain more zinc than any other food. Some other foods that contain zinc are red meats, nuts, and turkey.

Walnuts and turkey are examples of foods that contain important eyefood vitamins and minerals.

EAT HAM

What is an Omega-3 Fatty Acid?

Eating too much fat, especially the fat in unhealthy foods such as French fries, is not healthy. But did you know that certain types of fat are actually good for your body? Your body uses some fats as fuel. Fats also transport vitamins to your body parts, including your eyes. Omega-3 fatty acids are good fats that are important for eye health.

Eat eggs for your eyes! Egg yolk has lutein.

Fish contain omega-3 fatty acids. When you eat fish, your body receives the benefits of these healthy fatty acids. Two very important omega-3 fatty acids for your body are DHA (docosahexaenoic acid) and EPA (eicosapentaenoic acid). DHA and EPA are good for your brain, heart, skin, and especially your eyes.

What is a Carotenoid?

Carotenoids are **pigments** that give things color. Lutein and zeaxanthin are important carotenoids for humans. They are found in the retina of the eye. They help protect the retina from harmful UV and blue light. Your body cannot make lutein and zeaxanthin, so you need to get it from the food you eat.

Eye nutrition is an important part of healthy eyes. These vitamins and minerals are the most important ones for your eyes.

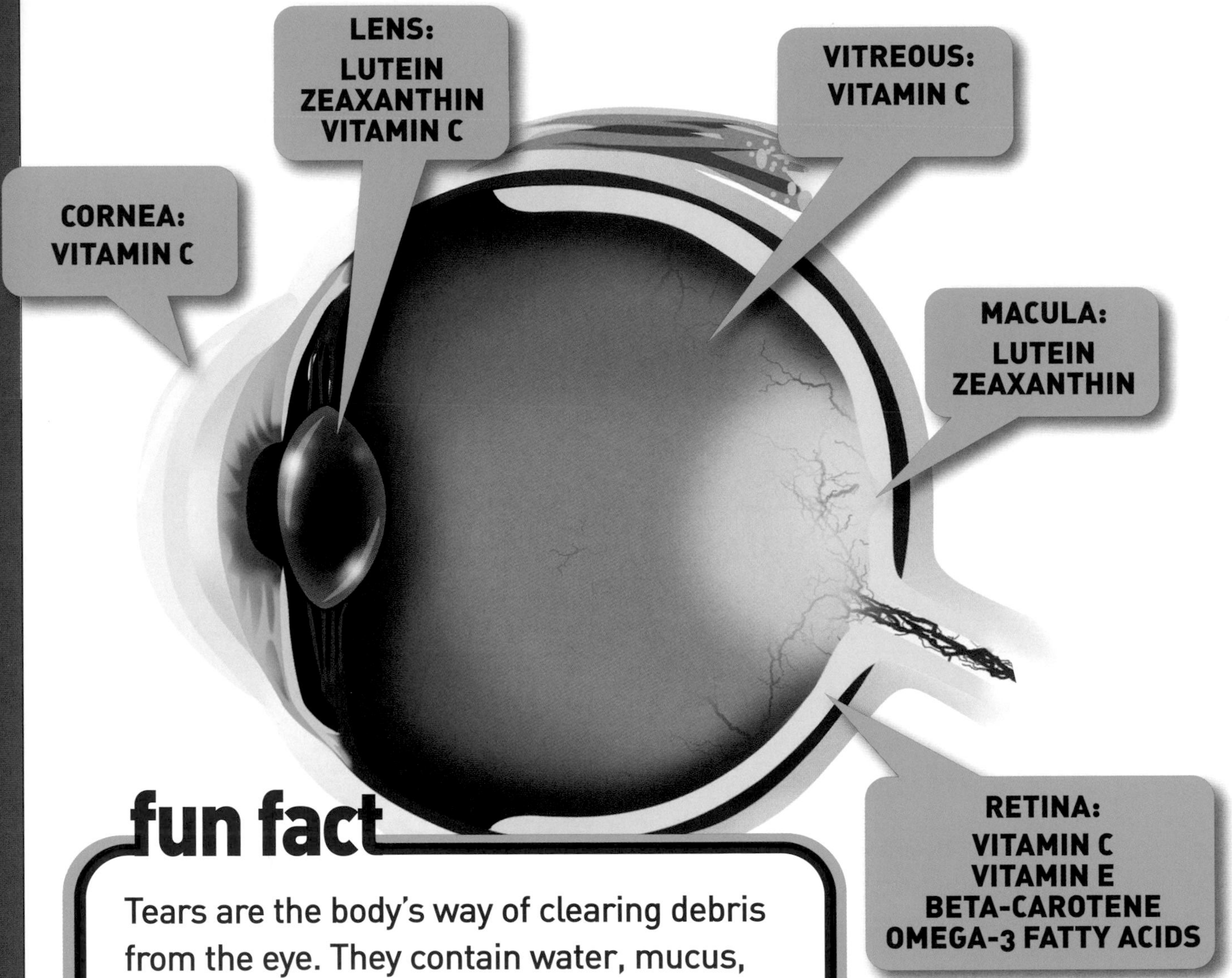

LENS:
LUTEIN
ZEAXANTHIN
VITAMIN C

VITREOUS:
VITAMIN C

CORNEA:
VITAMIN C

MACULA:
LUTEIN
ZEAXANTHIN

RETINA:
VITAMIN C
VITAMIN E
BETA-CAROTENE
OMEGA-3 FATTY ACIDS

fun fact

Tears are the body's way of clearing debris from the eye. They contain water, mucus, oil, and chemicals that can kill some germs.

VITAMIN or MINERAL	LOCATION IN EYE	FOUND IN FOODS SUCH AS
Lutein	macula, lens	leafy greens (kale, spinach), egg yolks, broccoli
Zeaxanthin	macula, lens	orange peppers, goji berries
Vitamin C	cornea, aqueous, vitreous, retina, lens	kiwi, all colored peppers, broccoli, citrus fruit
Vitamin E	retina	nuts, seeds, healthy oils (extra virgin olive oil), eggs, orange peppers, kiwi
Beta-Carotene	retina (The body makes vitamin A from beta-carotene)	sweet potatoes, squash, carrots
Omega-3 Fatty Acids: DHA, EPA	retina, meibomian glands (eyelids)	wild salmon, sardines, rainbow trout, light tuna
Zinc	Zinc is a mineral that is important in the functioning of the cells in the eye. It also helps bring vitamin A and vitamin E into the eye from other parts of the body.	oysters, turkey, lean red meat, nuts, whole grains

Recipes for Healthy Eyes

Kale chips for laser vision? Banana smoothie for seeing through walls? Okay, maybe these recipes won't give you superhero sight, but the superfoods they contain will make your eyes, and the rest of your body, strong and healthy.

Lip-Smacking Leafy Greens
Here are some creative ways to make and eat leafy greens:

Kale — kale chips. Kale is a vegetable with green or purple leaves that are packed with lutein and zeaxanthin. This makes it an eyefoods powerhouse. It also contains beta-carotene, vitamin C, vitamin E, zinc, and fiber.

Spinach — tastes great in a smoothie. Spinach has had a bad rap as a yucky, mushy vegetable, but fresh spinach is fantastic in salads and wraps.

Romaine lettuce — makes a great wrap. Romaine is a strong lettuce that can easily stand in for bread. Fill a leaf of romaine lettuce with egg salad for a tasty lunch.

KALE

SPINACH

ROMAINE LETTUCE

KALE CHIPS

How much should I eat?

Eyefoods Recommendations:
Eat leafy greens every day. One handful a day of leafy greens will give your eyes a lot of lutein and other important eye nutrients. You should also eat leafy greens both cooked and raw every week.

KALE CRUNCH CHIPS
Half a bunch of kale
Drizzle of olive oil
Pinch of salt

1. Ask an adult to preheat the oven to 350°F. Wash, then dry the kale in either a salad spinner or on a clean tea towel.

2. Tear the kale leaves into bite-sized pieces, discarding the tough central part.

3. Drizzle with a little olive oil and, working with your hands, rub the leaves gently so all of the kale has a light coating of oil.

4. Place on a baking sheet in one layer. Sprinkle a pinch of salt over the kale.

5. Ask an adult to put the baking sheet in the oven. Allow to bake for 20 minutes. Watch the kale to make sure it does not burn.

6. Have an adult remove the baking sheet from the oven when the leaves are crispy. Enjoy!

Eye-Power Smoothies

Smoothies are a spectacular way to get all the vitamins and nutrients your eyes need in one deliciously drinkable form. They are fun to make, too!

COW MANURE SMOOTHIE
    1 banana
    1 cup mixed berries
    3 cups spinach
    1½ cups cold water

1. Put all the ingredients in a blender.
2. Blend until smooth. Enjoy at once or store in the refrigerator for up to three days.

PEACH POWER SMOOTHIE
2 cups frozen peaches
1 cup baby spinach
½ cup green grapes
1 cup water

1. Put all the ingredients in a blender.

2. Blend until smooth. Enjoy at once or store in the refrigerator for up to three days.

PINEAPPLE PASSION SMOOTHIE
1 cup pineapple
1 cup light coconut milk or coconut water (available in supermarkets)
3 cups baby spinach

1. Ask an adult to prepare one cup of cut-up pineapple.

2. Put in a blender and add the other ingredients.

3. Blend until smooth. Enjoy at once or store in the refrigerator for up to three days.

GREEN GOODNESS SMOOTHIE
1 banana
1 cup honeydew melon
1 tablespoon lime juice
3 cups baby spinach
1 cup cold water

1. Ask an adult to prepare one cup of cut-up honeydew melon.

2. Put in a blender with the banana.

3. Add the lime juice, then the spinach and water.

4. Blend until smooth. Enjoy at once or store in the refrigerator for up to three days.

Peppers are an eyefood that are both tasty and terrific for sight. Orange peppers are very good for your eyes because they contain a lot of zeaxanthin.

What is zeaxanthin?

Zeaxanthin (zee-axe-anthin) is a cousin of lutein. It is an orange-red pigment found in the center of the macula. Zeaxanthin gives paprika, saffron, and goji berries their orange color.

All colored peppers are good for your eyes, but orange peppers are the best for eye health because they contain a lot of zeaxanthin.

Creative ways to eat orange peppers:

1. Make an orange pepper boat and fill it with chicken, turkey, tuna, or salmon.
2. Make fresh juice with an electric juicer, using orange peppers and cantaloupe.
3. Enjoy orange pepper slices with your favorite healthy dip such as hummus (chick-pea dip) or Tzatziki (yogurt and cucumber dip).

SALMON PEPPER BOATS

ORANGE PEPPER CANTALOUPE JUICE

ORANGE PEPPER BOATS WITH SALMON SALAD

 1 can wild salmon, no skin, no bones
 2 orange peppers
 2 green onions, finely chopped
 1 kale leaf, finely chopped

DRESSING

 2 tbsp non-fat Greek yogurt
 1 tbsp fresh dill, finely chopped
 1 tbsp lemon juice, plus the zest of the lemon, finely grated
 Sea salt and fresh ground pepper

Makes 2 servings

1. To make the dressing, mix all the ingredients in a small bowl. Set aside.
2. Drain the salmon. Crumble it into flakes in a medium sized bowl. Mix in green onion, kale, and enough dressing to coat. Season to taste with salt and pepper.
3. Remove seeds and white membrane of orange peppers and cut into 2-inch thick wedges. Make sure your cuts correspond to the bumpy sides, so you end up with hollow boats.
4. Spoon the salmon mixture into the pepper wedges.

See-Food

Fish are fantastic for sight! They are tasty and packed with the fatty acids your eyes need for health. The healthiest eyefoods fish include wild Alaskan salmon, rainbow trout, sardines, mackerel, and light tuna.

Fish come from all kinds of water. Some fish are ocean dwellers or salt water fish. Fresh water fish live in lakes and rivers. Fish are also grouped by temperature and the depth of the water they inhabit, such as cold water, tropical water, shallow water, and deep water. Cold water fish have different amounts of nutrients than fish from tropical water because of their diet.

Fish contain the healthy omega-3 fatty acids DHA and EPA. DHA and EPA are important for your eyes, as well as your brain, heart, and skin.

ALGAE

KRILL

Eating fish gives your body more DHA and EPA than any other food. So, it's important to eat cold water fish two times per week. You can also eat other foods to get even more DHA for your body. Some other foods are enriched with omega-3 fatty acids, such as omega-3 eggs and yogurt.

Algae get energy from sunlight, are eaten by krill, which are, in turn eaten by some fish.

FISH

How do omega-3s (DHA and EPA) keep our eyes healthy?

1. Omega-3s keep your tears healthy so your eyes stay moist.
2. Omega-3s protect your retina from age-related macular degeneration (AMD), a disease that causes gradual blindness.
3. Omega-3s help your body absorb lutein and zeaxanthin, as well as other nutrients important for your eyes.

Fish is a healthy food, but some types of fish should be eaten less frequently because of the threat of **contamination** from chemicals such as mercury and PCBs (polychlorinated biphenyls).

Smaller fish are cleaner than large fish. Small fish do not contain harmful levels of contaminants such as mercury. Examples of small fish are sardines and mackerel.

fun fact

In Japan and other countries where people eat a lot fish, there are fewer cases of eye disease such as macular degeneration.

Fish for Dinner!

MANGO TANGO SALMON

4 wild Alaskan salmon fillets
(Frozen or fresh)
1 tbsp olive oil
Salt and pepper

MANGO SALSA

1 cup frozen mango, cut into
¼-inch cubes
1 cup grape tomatoes, cut in half
½ orange pepper, cut in ¼-inch
cubes (eat the rest as a snack)
1 green onion, finely chopped
Salt and pepper
Juice and zest of one lime
1 tbsp olive oil

Prepare salsa

1. Mix mango, tomatoes, orange peppers, and green onion in a medium sized bowl. Season with a little salt and pepper.

2. In a small bowl, whisk together the olive oil, lime zest and lime juice. Pour it over the salsa and let it sit.

Cook salmon

1. Ask an adult to preheat the oven's broiler to 400°F or max. Line a cooking sheet with aluminum foil.

2. Place the fish fillets on the cooking sheet and brush with olive oil. Sprinkle a little salt and pepper on each fillet.

3. Have an adult place the cooking sheet in the oven for about 10 to 15 minutes. When the salmon is brown on top and firm in the middle, ask an adult to remove it.

4. Top salmon with some salsa and serve with a green salad and brown rice.

Serves 4

Eggs are "eggsellent" for your eyes because egg yolk is loaded with lutein. Certain eggs even contain omega-3 fatty acids. Eggs also contain vitamin E, which is important for healthy eyes.

How much should I eat?

Eyefoods Recommendations:
Eat four eggs per week. Sunny-side up, easy over, poached, boiled, scrambled, or in an omelet, these are all tasty ways to enjoy eggs.

Tips: Add baby spinach to scrambled eggs or an omelet, they will load your eyes with lutein.

Add a boiled egg to a green salad made with baby spinach or romaine lettuce.

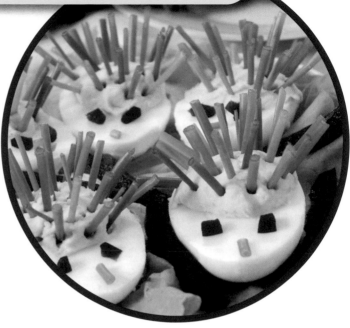

Deviled egg hedgehogs made with chives for hair are tasty treats.

fun fact

Eggs for Dogs
Eggs can help improve your pet's eyesight too! Plus, they help make your dog's coat healthy and shiny.

Whole grains are grains that have not been **refined**, or have not had the outer layer removed. They contain more fiber and many more nutrients than refined grains. Fiber is the part of the plant that the body cannot digest or absorb. It is pushed through the **digestive system** and helps the bowel get rid of waste. In other words, it helps you poop. Examples of whole grains include whole wheat bread, rolled oats, oatmeal, whole wheat pasta, barley, brown rice, and quinoa.

It is important to eat whole grains instead of refined grains to keep your eyes and your entire body healthy.

White bread, white rice, and white pasta are all refined grains. This means that they have been milled and processed to remove their fiber and all of the nutrients that are contained in the husk of the grain.

To make this tasty muesli, mix together equal parts rolled oats, skim milk, and yogurt. Wait 30 minutes or overnight. Top with fruit or nuts. Enjoy!

43

All fruits and vegetables are good for you, but some are better for your eyes than others. Vegetables such as broccoli, Brussels sprouts, sweet potatoes, carrots, green beans and peas are especially important for healthy eyes.

Vitamin C is a very important vitamin for our bodies and for our eyes. It is found in all parts of our eyes. As well as keeping our eyes healthy, vitamin C helps keep the **immune system** healthy.

Our bodies do not make vitamin C. We cannot store vitamin C either. To get it, we have to eat foods that are high in vitamin C several times a day.

For a fun party treat, make an "orange bowl" and fill it with cut up kiwi and citrus.

Juice

One-hundred percent pure juice usually contains a lot of vitamin C, however, it can also contain a lot of sugar. So, it's important not to drink more than one serving or a half a cup of juice per day.

Foods high in vitamin C include kiwi, orange, red, yellow and green peppers, oranges, grapefruits, and broccoli.

fun fact

Most animals can make vitamin C in their bodies. Like humans, guinea pigs don't make vitamin C. If you have a guinea pig as a pet, feed them red peppers, kale, and broccoli for vitamin C.

Be Active and Give it a Rest

To keep your body and eyes healthy, it is important to be active for at least one hour every day. You don't have to get all your exercise at once. You can spread it out through the day. Try walking or riding your bike more often. Just about any form of active play will be good for your health — and your eyes!

Exercise Your Eyes

You can exercise your eyes, too! Eye exercises can help strengthen your eye muscles. Try this exercise: Sit down in your bedroom or the family room of your home. Focus your eyes on an object about 20 feet away from you. Then focus on an object right in front of you. Move your eyes back and forth between the objects without moving your head. Do this 10 times. Was it hard to focus?

Physical activity is good for your eyes. Always remember to stretch your muscles after you exercise.

Protecting Your Eyes: Give Them A Rest

When you use a computer, read a book, or play video games, you blink less — sometimes as little as five times per minute. Humans normally blink every two to five seconds. Blinking washes debris away from the eyeball and keeps your eyes lubricated. The intense focusing on a computer screen or video game can cause your eyes to become dry, **irritated**, and tired. Eye care experts suggest the 20-20-20 rule. Every 20 minutes look at something 20 feet away for 20 seconds. This will help give your eyes a break.

Give your eyes a rest and take a break from playing video games.

Glossary

cells The basic, and smallest, structural unit of all living things

challenging Something that is difficult

comprehensive Complete

contamination Something that is not pure

digestive system The bodily system that breaks down food

distort Something that is twisted out of shape, or difficult to see

extraocular muscles A group of six muscles that control the movement of the eye

immune system The system within the body that provides resistance to and fights diseases and infections

inflammation When a part of the body is irritated and swollen

irritated Pain or discomfort

nourishment The food or substances needed for health and to keep the body in good condition

nutrients Substances that provide nourishment for growth and health

pigments Natural substances that are colored or give color

prescription Instructions, including medicines or tools, that are given by a doctor to treat a medical condition

refined Food that is processed and less natural

three dimensions Seeing the length, breadth, and depth of something all at the same time

Index